MY THOUGHTS

SERIES 2

LEONARD DENIS

Series : Two

MY THOUGHTS

MY THOUGHTS

THANK YOU

Mom, Geraldine dad, and siblings, who encouraged me to indulge in my education . I spent many long car rides creating epic tales to write to give you my own views and thoughts . Rik ,Shizz , The block and David Gaston , my childhood friends who enjoy my eclectic ways and provide great suggestions.
Nawaal and Briana Sumpter, who patiently listened to my stories and never judged me. Earlson Satine, who inspired me daily to reach for my dreams and to aim for the stars. Sabrina, Jamarl, Kirstin Lewis, Tony Henley , Greg and Dorian who provided insightful feedback to help my polishing efforts.

R&H /Sound Hustlaz for their feedback and
enthusiastic support. Nicole Benns
and Janice C. Davis who offered great advice!
& renewed my love of writing .
My sons, Lj Zahir and Peyton-Alexander
Denis.. I do this for you.
To everyone that ever doubted me Thank
you !!!!
Book two

Thank you God,
Read on,

NIGHTMARE

I watched the Bill Cosby trial saving
R.kelly and this is My thoughts...
To be raped is to be broken, in more ways
than You could ever count. To be raped is
to have somebody reach inside to your
soul, and force it to slowly die. Have you
ever had somebody grab your hand, maybe
playfully at first, but then hold on just a
little too tightly, and for a moment you
realize you're not strong enough to break
free and just have to wait for your hand to
be released? It's a common scenario,
something that happens all the time on the
preschool playground, starting all the way
from playful childhood. Imagine that
feeling, that moment where you realize

you aren't strong enough to break free when that person grabs your wrist, and imagine that feeling applied to your whole body. Your arms, legs, voice, everything... become useless. Your body isn't even your body anymore. It belongs to them. And not only your body, but everything you are is exposed and ripped away from you. And there's nothing for you to do except wait. At some point, you stop struggling, or maybe you never even could, paralyzed by fear or alcohol. And you feel as though anything in the world could be better than this. Even death. You may even pray that you could choose death instead. Unfortunately, you couldn't, and every second that passed felt like an hour, excruciating hour by excruciating hour.

I personally never been rapped but i was with someone who was rapped in her younger years.

She never got over it, and never did nothing about it

She would tell me she would actually see the guy in passing and she would freak out. I felt bad angry and helpless at the same time as much as i told her not to blame herself, things i told her to uplift her .. getting rapped temporarily put her in a sunken place, I alone couldn't get her out. Though I'm not with the person anymore it made me feel for everyone who ever been a victim of sexual violence. I used to hate law and order svu because of the officers discretion on their un-subs , but i understood his passion for woman of vulnerability. To any lady reading this it's okay to fight and take a stand about topics like this. People need to be aware, and to know it's not right. We should all be unified to find the solution. I don't want broken little girls becoming broken down woman

EXPECTATIONS

....

VERSUS TRUST

I don't believe we have the right to expect anything from anyone. Some people have difficulty with that concept – especially in intimate relationships. They get confused with the difference between expectations and trust.

An expectation is a strong belief that something will happen or will be the case in the future or a belief that someone will or should do something. If we apply that to any relationship, it sets us up for failure.
You think someone not going to lie , cheat or hide things he or she is expected not to?

Expectations are resentments waiting to happen. Trust, on the other hand is a firm belief in the reliability, truth, ability, or strength of someone or something. I liken trust to faith. It's accepted without the need for evidence or investigation. However, in a healthy relationship, trust is built slowly. A pattern is developed over time that shows one that the other is trustworthy. Those who trust too much, too soon are either confusing trust with expectations, or they are afraid to let the relationship take its normal course. Either way, they find themselves in a lot of pain they could probably avoid if they could learn to be patient and allow the relationship to evolve.

I had this on girl I broke her trust and not only that, It made her question other people that she trusted in the process.
The expectations I believe in her mind was she was loyal to me so she thought it would be reciprocated back-but not everyone thinks or perceive thing the same with expectations.
When trust is broken, it can be rebuilt, but it takes long-term, consistent effort – sometimes extreme effort – to prove trustworthiness again. Once that process has begun, then the other side must eventually begin to trust again – a little at a time. Both parties must be diligent in rebuilding

trust. When that's done, the relationship will never be the same – but it is often better.

TREAT HER LIKE A PERSON

NOT A WOMAN!

Women are different, weird, emotional and also more annoying than men , so you need to treat them accordingly. But they don't know that they're different from real me (they're "difficult ," after all), so I found out you have to work around that.

First… you can't approach women as women… don't treat her like a lady, treat her like a person, this sounds funny but hear me out- women need more time, they ask more questions… get to know what motivates her, her passions her dreams … if you connect with her on that level, not on the basis of her gender, then she's really going to dig you. pretend like you're treating her like an individual, but know that what you're really dealing with is a female species that named a woman

Second… girls triangulate, women seek many sources of opinions .. in other words "bitches talk" just know she's gonna do that, why don't you play along… give her other sources of information that augment the advice that you're giving her… that's a good way to play to women's natural ability and need to triangulate on advice that they're getting. She's gonna do it anyway, put that to your advantage.

Third… Be honest in a harsh way! Woman always say the want the truth but they can't handle it . No one should have trust really in anyone just expectations. No ones perfect so there are times you may not meet them , once you get a woman to agree on that.. why lie? She know you'll bound to fuck up sometimes.. she may even forgive you faster ,

MY SOULMATE

Each "failed" relationship has given me clues about what i want in my ideal partner. The problem is, many women and men focus on the negative instead of the positive

We all as social creatures have a deep and underlying desire to find that one perfect person to spend the rest of our days with. That one person when you meet, you feel an uncontrollable attraction to and an illogical sense of familiarity with. As if you've known that person for a lifetime, or perhaps lifetimes. Whatever you want to call it, films and TV series alike have romanticized the phenomenon known as the soulmate

The good news is, if you know what you don't want, you know what you *do* want. Your power to create lies in your ability to choose thoughts that are positively clear so that you can tell the universe exactly what you desire. (*"I want a man who puts me first and loves me unconditionally."*)

You can tell if your affirmation is positive or negative by the way it makes you feel. If it makes you feel great, it is positive. If it makes you feel bad, it is negative. It's that simple. If you find yourself thinking negative thoughts, simply turn them around and start focusing on the positive. You will immediately feel better and you will be in alignment with love. I don't know if I'll ever find my soul mate: heck I've been i love before but, to find someone who equally
Loves you the way you love them is very difficult.

I dated a teacher once who went to the university of Villanova she was also a cheerleader too. The way we "connect " early on you'd think we'd be destined for a whole life together but fate had a slightly different plan.

Right now, my soulmate is myself. That's the only person that i didn't create that i truly love inside and out, i finally taught myself the essence of self-love. When you love yourself, you become more genuine. You don't try to hide behind the things-that-will-make-people-like-me facade. You know the fact that you can never please everyone and so you don't.
Loving yourself will make you appreciate when it's time to love your soulmate

When you love yourself, you become stronger. You learn how to fight when you have to. You know the difference between giving up and knowing when to stop fighting. You become more connected with your emotions and you know that being strong does not necessarily mean you can't cry.
By me achieving this i know now when the time comes, I'll be ready to receive my soulmate :::
and the only reason why ..? Is because i learned how to truly love myself first

PERCEPTION

The way in which you perceive people is the way they are likely to be. People act according to expectations. If you expect someone to be mad they will energetically and subconsciously feel this and more than likely act in relation to your expectation. Think about an intimate relationship. How many times have you visualized a scenario you didn't want to happen come true? For instance, "I get the feeling they are not that in to me;" "since they are not calling they must not really want to see me;" and "I bet they are hiding something." I have been on both sides of this scenario several times. It is clear that an insecure frame of reference creates disconnection in the relationship which usually leads to cheating, arguments then later on a breaking up. It is easy to feel this insecure energy from the other person. As the person fearing loss it also becomes apparent that insecurity exists in your mind before it manifests in the relationship. The fear of losing someone causes enough anxiety that your thoughts become expectations that they will leave. The other person is always confused in the beginning saying, "I totally like you, why do you feel this way?" Eventually the other person acts in accordance with your expectation (perception).

In order to improve a relationship you must evolve your perception of the other person to the place you want to see them in. If you see this person as mean and you want to see them nice then picture them nice. You will relate to and treat this person according to how you see them. If you see them mean you will respond to them as if they are mean keeping them in this label. This makes it more difficult for them to evolve out of this label when everyone around them keeps picturing them there. When you see them as nice you will become more aware and appreciative of all the nice things they do. As you respond with praise and positive emotion you are reinforcing a nicer personality to emerge from them. You are changing them by changing your perception.

I was in a "situation "and i started dating another woman . The other woman knew about my situation but she really didn't speak much about it . One day i invited over and things got a little intimate . To me that was a great thing but in all reality it was that day that changed the whole perception of how this girl viewed me months to come . Eventually i did end that first "situation " and my whole focus was this new girl. I really liked this girl a lot, she was very colorful smart and she could dress. One of my dearest friends knew her so she was official to the squad. I wanted to make it official with her but it was always something holding her back.

You MY THOUGHTS.....Her perception of me being sneaky, or even untrustworthy.

If someone knows that you cheated on someone with them ,why would that person ever trust or take you seriously? At the time i didn't think of that . I just had the perception of her being my girl and me being the best i can be for her. The worst thing in life is to have someone perceive you negatively because that's a perception that's very hard to erase . Hey

Interlude……

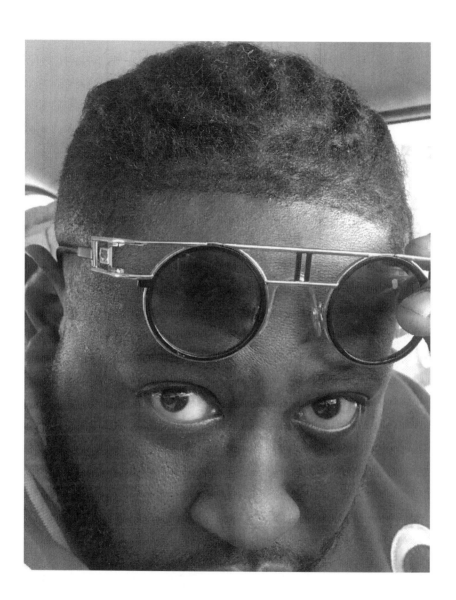

BOOST MY EGO

I know this girl, who spends a lot of her day wondering what
her boyfriend is doing, looking for clues that he loves her, wondering why he isn't paying attention to her, worrying that he's flirting with other girls on Instagram
She's not happy in this relationship — she's dependent on him for her happiness, and unhappy when he's not providing the validation she needs, when he doesn't show how much he loves her. She's insecure, jealous, needy. This doesn't make for a good relationship, or a happy person.
What happens when you have some degree of this in your relationship? You're not a good

boyfriend, girlfriend, spouse. The other person feels like he (or she) has to keep making you happy, always be "on point " so that you won't wonder what's wrong with your relationship, always supply your needs, never have the freedom to do their own thing while you do yours. This makes for a tough relationship, and if it lasts more than a few years, long-term problems usually develop.

I know, because I've done it myself, and had to learn the hard way that this doesn't work well. Almost everyone I know who has had relationship problems has had some of these same issues. The people who have healthy long-term relationships ... they've found a way to be whole, independent, secure.

When you're whole, you don't need someone else's validation to be happy — because you accept yourself. You don't need someone else to love you in order to feel loved — because you love yourself. That's not to say you don't love to be loved by others, or want others in your life — but you already provide the foundation of what you need, all by yourself, by accepting and loving yourself.

When you're whole, you are not insecure, because you aren't worried so much about the other person leaving. Sure, it would be a great loss for your loved one to abandon you, but you'd be fine on your own. You wouldn't be "alone" because you have the best company in the world — yourself. You know you'd survive, be happy, do great things, even without that person. That's not to say you don't want your lover to stay — but you aren't always afraid of the possibility of that person leaving.

When you're whole, you don't need the other person to check in with you all the time, because you're happy on your own. You're OK if they go do their own thing, because you're secure in your relationship and you're perfectly fine doing your own thing too. You don't need reassurance of that person's love, because you're secure.

This took me a very hard time to get and to manifests in my everyday life. I'm a man, and i don't care what anyone says assurance is an ego boost and when your significant other doesn't articulate that affection well with you , you'll tend to feel "some type of way" , insecure or may have a bruised ego.

I knew this couple that i grew up with in my neighborhood. they were young starting off but very much happy with each other. the girl, was very ambitious, sophisticated and out going had one problem.. she had a care free life. Even though her and her guy friend didn't claim each other they were pretty much boyfriend and girlfriend. One day while she was sleep he looked at her phone and seen text messages and other things about her dealing with someone else.. to any man, if you're smashing a woman you really like , "those buns belong to you" (regardless if you're together or not)and if you find out she gave it to someone else. Sometime insecurity start playing a part because of a mans busied ego. What happened to this couple is the guy started doing him and even though he was hurt the only way he dealt with the Hurt was to hurt her ten times worse. My thoughts... if she would of always made him feel secure he would of never went through her phone.

Always make your other half feel wanted even if it sound repetitive. You don't know how much it could brighten his day or a. Relationship

BEING VULNERABLE

Ever felt terrified to tell a boyfriend or girlfriend how much you needed their help or support? Or perhaps you've avoided bringing up an issue because you didn't want to seem inadequate or unlovable .

All of these reactions can arise when we feel vulnerable in relationships,

There was a time in my young life .. i was a radical and didn't care about anything but myself, i meet this girl at a cookout i wasn't even on her she was cute but, she wasn't feeling my swag until she got drunk, nonetheless we exchanged numbers and started hanging out. We hit it off and dated a while and i never knew how i truly felt for her until i kissed her passionately. I remember the day like it was yesterday, i don't remember what i had on but she had on a blue romper and was looking like a jawn . I kissed her next to the water and it was all she wrote .

Kissing for everyone feels differently, it depends on who that person is but for someone like me- it's a very big thing to kiss someone and that to kiss someone I didn't even know love. was crazy!... the best feelings comes in heart because the heart is not reactive like the body. The heart is not logical like the brain., the heart only feels and experience the reality, truth & purity of love. love feels happy ... to experience the acceptance by someone you love the most. Is scary and satisfying .

I hated being in a relationship when i felt vulnerable, i felt like a sucker and everything i did wasn't good enough because she was my kryptonite . being in a bind with my health i was afraid to show people i was vulnerable. Fuck that. I never wanted to let someone feel pity for me. I did let some in but i still felt weak. I always thought being Vulnerable to a person was a bad thing I've learned it is a necessity in life. Being vulnerable at times makes you feel like your powerless and you've giving your power to someone else.

I had to grow up. I was not vulnerable ,I was just scared of growth and understanding .

Human beings are the only creatures who do not attain adulthood automatically. A baby chick has no choice but to turn into a chicken. But the world is full of people psychologically stuck in childhood and adolescence, no matter how old they happen to be. For us, to mature is a decision; adulthood is an achievement, one that requires—and results—in personal power.

This can take decades, but it starts with a vision of the "core self." This is the part of you that connects to reality, placing you at the center of experiences that you personally create. To have a core self is to be the author of your own story; it is the exact opposite of being a victim, who must live a life authored by others .

I hade to start loving myself ,put god in my life and also tell others to embrace and be vulnerable for the ones that you love and will ride for you.These escape routes all lead back to the person i really am, and i know what really counts and that extends far beyond the individual: the glory of creation, the beauty of nature, the heart qualities of love and compassion, the mental power to discover new things, and those unexpected epiphanies that bring the presence of God these universal aspects are our true source of power. They are you, and you are all of them. The path out of feeling vulnerable, reaching for the goal of invulnerability, is opened inside yourself

To ladies that have baby father drama, god is great never let a man steal your power you are loved . To men that are scared to stand up to a woman , grow a pair (haha) no, honestly be wise and love life.

The thing that makes you grand is the power you possess. Never lose it

FALSE HOPE

....

Man this thing used to bother me ; False hope in dating. We've all been or had an experience in this first hand . I used to want a chick so bad that i held on to every little inch of whatever shorty gave me , hoping to give it more meaning than is there. That shit was built around fantasies and wishful thinking. I used to be like "damn- why am i wasting my time? Why do we hold hope in dating when i could be out there finding something better? I've asked myself the same question over and over again . False hope, is dangerous.
Why so?

- You become obsessed with the person, their actions, their whereabouts and their life in general

- You over analyze every word they say and action you experience from them looking for hidden meanings to demonstrate what you want to hear

- You manipulate situations to turn them in your favor where they are involved

- Even though they haven't really committed to you, you keep holding out for the day that they will

- You don't give a chance to potentially great matches because you want to be available for when your love finally decides to make it official

- You compromise your own needs for theirs and would be willing to give up your values for them

- You develop a hero complex and want to save them

- Your pride goes out the window

- You would do anything for them … they say jump and you say how high

- You think that you can't get better or don't deserve better than them

False hope in dating occurs when it really is one sided. They aren't really interested in an actual official relationship with you or in being with you in any real way. They've told you this but you don't believe them. You just want to believe so hard that they'll come around. Let me save you the grief, waiting around is only hurting you and not them. If they wanted to be with you they would be.

WHAT'S LIKABLE

PROGRESS IS DANCING TO THE
SAME SONG YOU USED TO CRY TO.

Many times in life we are at crossroads and we
wonder which direction to head in. We are

mammals of habit, and tend to want to stay in something and hold onto that which is known and familiar, even if it's not the right fit for our lives anymore. Our future decisions are based on what we have established as "my type", or "my habit", or "my known preference". There's nothing wrong in having comfort zones, be it food, types of relationships or personal routines. But, what's important is to know is that the reason you are at a crossroad is because something needs to change..

Saying goodbye to people, places, and things in our lives can be a mixed bag of emotions. Sometimes these endings leave us feeling relieved and excited for the next stage to come. Others fill us with sadness as we reluctantly or abruptly are forced to move on with our life. And at times what we leave behind causes us to feel both extremes.

Whether it's changing jobs or dealing with a break-up, closing a chapter in life can be both difficult and joyous . Writing my first book everyone was asking me about the red head girl. Who is she?, did i ever speak to her again? Did i tell her she was talked about in a book? I guess as much as i spoke about me being over it and more matured about the situation, you can tell

by my writing, the chapter wasn't fully closed.
The real reason why i felt that way was: i felt
like i was getting played, she had other "friends
" i was never her top priority. I never knew how
she felt then and all i got was " you were fine
answer" .
I wanted to know why. Why wasn't i giving the
same opportunities others had to win her heart.
& If she truly did love me why couldn't she ever
show it? Was she ashamed of me? Was i
someone her friends shouldn't know about?
All those insecurities and doubts i had was
important to focus on using those experiences as
a way to better myself . God knows the plans He
has for us, and those plans are for us to prosper,
have hope, and a future (Jeremiah 29:11). We
have to trust God's word. If we truly seek His
face, will, and direction then He will direct our
path (Proverbs 3:6).
Not all reflection is a bad thing. We shouldn't
ignore our past; it is what formed us into the
person we are today . I did speak to the red head
girl again we had a very intimate conversation.
We are friends again and certain things at that
time i didn't get i guess i understand now.

One thing that she won't ever let go, is me sleeping with her friend (even though we never was in a committed relationship)

I don't dwell on the past i reflect on it . The difference between dwelling versus reflecting on the past is that reflecting is looking back to move forward. It means asking yourself what you learned from your experience. What could I have done better or differently? What does this chapter show me about myself? What can I take away from this experience? Reflection is a contemplative and intentional thought-process that analyzes and digests events in a way that helps us to learn from them.

I can't say she hasn't done that because our conversations and just entire interaction is mostly improved from the last encounters.

Will we have a romance relationship? I'm not sure .The future is a blank page staring us in the face waiting for us to leave our mark. God gives us opportunities, and we should seize them. Hebrews 12:1 says, "Let us run with endurance the race God has set before us." Sometimes we don't understand why we are where we are, but we can take confidence in knowing that God is by our side. He will never leave us nor forsake us (Deuteronomy 31:6).

There is a reason why my homie reached out to her and got her to reply to me . There's a reason why we're friends and there is a reason why i adore her and what god has in store for me
So, the next time you find yourself waving goodbye, take a glance in the rearview mirror of life, appreciate the view for a moment, and then enjoy the ride onto roads untraveled. Who knows who you will meet, how God will use you, or where you will end up.

EMBRACING YOU

....

I never considered my self an ugly person: but i just never considered myself a person that wasn't a heartthrob though.

Growing up how you look is never defined on how you view yourself but how society sees you. If you're not slim your considered fat , if your black and dark skinned your considers black as shit .i grew up as a dark skinned kid from Brooklyn who parents who happened to be Haitian. You know what that mean? I was called every or any derogatory name because of my skin and ethnicity . People i knew grew up with the assumption being black was ugly and since i was an another nationality, i was considered lowest of the low and not knowing who i really am . There is perhaps nothing more perplexing than realizing one day that you've lost yourself. It's that feeling of not knowing who you are, not being sure of what you like, and not knowing who you want to become. "Who am I?" becomes a daily question that never seems to be answered. The good news is that you are not alone. Everyone, at some point in their life, is pushed into the whirlwind of personal crisis. But the question remains, "How do you find yourself when you don't know who you are?" The greatest and most important adventure of our lives is discovering who we really are. Yet, so many of us walk around either not really knowing or listening to an awful inner critic that gives us all the wrong ideas about ourselves Finding yourself may sound like an inherently self-centered goal, but it is actually an unselfish process that is at the root of everything we do in life. In order to be the most valuable person to the world around us, the best partner, parent etc, we have to first know who we are, what we

value and, in effect, what we have to offer. This personal journey is one every individual will benefit from taking. It is a process that involves breaking down – shedding layers that do not serve us in our lives and don't reflect who we really are. Yet, it also involves a tremendous act of building up – recognizing who we want to be and passionately going about fulfilling our unique destiny – whatever that may be. It's a matter of recognizing our personal power, yet being open and vulnerable to our experiences. It isn't something to fear or avoid, berating ourselves along the way, but rather something to seek out with the curiosity and compassion we would have toward a fascinating new friend.,
I took on a lot of steps for me to embrace who i am now
Here are some of them

1. Make sense of your past
In order to uncover who we are and why we act the way we do, we have to know our own story. Being brave and willing to explore our past is an important stepping stone on the road to understanding ourselves and becoming who we want to be. I used to blame everyone for my

fuck ups, my bad relationships, my inconsistency of being a friend. I had to look in the mirror and take accountability for the bad and agree within that i wanted to change i wanted to be a person that was nearly perfect in the things i mentioned above (in a good way) Unresolved traumas my history inform the way i used to act. Never knew why my parents had a falling out when i was younger , why a girl was so into me in the beginning then cheat or fall back from me, or even i had i people considered good friends stab me in the back. The attitudes and atmosphere we grew up in have a heavy hand on how we act as adults.

Those situations can make a person bitter forever and i was for a while . Another examples can make you alter who you really are too . For example, having a harsh parent may have caused us to feel more guarded. We may grow up always feeling on the defense or resistant to trying new challenges for fear of being ridiculed.

My dad was a harsh dude- I laughed now cause then i used to hate how he was but respect the way he was . I had the balance of a harsh father and a cool as mom it balanced me in a way that i was never a defensive child but more of a "oh well" Type of guy but also made me a really really shy person up until today . When we try to cover up or hide from our past experiences, we can feel lost and like we don't really know ourselves. We may take actions automatically without asking why. There's reasons why your angry, scared to take risks, always defensive, always negative. It's because of your past. By acknowledging that We can then start to consciously separate from the more harmful influences from our history and actively alter our behavior to reflect how we really think and feel and how we choose to be in the crazy world.

2 . Seek a Meaning

You know, like-what's the meaning of life... haha,

No but honestly, seek out our own personal sense of purpose. This means separating your own point of view from other people's expectations of you . It means asking ourselves what your values are, what truly matters to you, then following the principles you. believe in. When i told people i wanted to be a writer , the laughed , one person told me it was impossible because my length of education, some just put my dream down and said i should focus on computers and not writing. Being a teacher, well teaching has always been my thing . I always wanted people to learn from me and my experience whatever the message was to "teach" i was all in for it . As a society many of us fall too easily into victimized thoughts and complaints about our circumstances and surroundings rather than orienting ourselves toward positive goals, strategies and solutions. Put simply, we think a lot about what we don't want instead of concentrating on what we do want to .

3. Be humble
Mahatma Gandhi once said "The best way to find yourself is to lose yourself in the service of others."

generosity can enhance one's sense of purpose, giving our lives more value and meaning . Giving knowledge or "dropping jewels I like to call it , gave me a sense of belonging. It was like everything i went through had a lesson I could pass on to others good and bad

4 Choose Wisely The Company You Keep

I wish we could choose our family : we don't , but often, we assume that the family you're born in defines who we are. While as children, we have little say in where we spend our time, throughout our lives we can choose who and what we want to be like . As adults, we can create a family of choice. We can seek out people who make us happy, who support what lights us up and who inspire us to feel passionate about our lives. This family may, of course, include people we are related to, but it's a family we've really chosen, a core group of people who we consider true allies and friends. Creating this family is a key component in finding ourselves, because who we choose to surround ourselves with has a profound effect on how we relate in the world. Don't have friends that won't support you. I had friends i cut off just cause they wouldn't support my book my organization or anything i would do. If was sad that complete strangers would give me support way more then the people i swore that was family and had my back. Having a support system that believes in us helps us in realizing our goals and developing on a personal level.

FAKE
LOVE

....

Single is always defined as "never been married, divorced, or are widowed." That means that almost half of us aren't committed or in "love", so it's silly to be sad about not being in a relationship right now. Only 57% of us are married and that isn't even a high number; it's like getting an F- on a test. Marriage is a social construct and there's really no reason to do paperwork and pay all that money just to say you love someone.

To find a true lover who can give you real love, you have to know what true love is. To attract and keep him/her, you have to give a genuine love in return. Knowing how to distinguish pure love from false love will give you wisdom on how to build a long-lasting relationship and avoid the toxic ones. Such insight will also keep you away from futile suffering due to loving the wrong person. Moreover, it will prevent you from hurting people and being guilty for not giving the right love. Maaaan... I'm not going to lie. Men lie a-lot . Growing up on bouvier st i had an old head named J the bodyguard. Jay was the man when it came to the girls him and Sampson. As a teen we used to mimic everything these two did because they always had girls running in and out of the house on the block. When we used to asked them how they get the girls they said "all we do is tell these birdies we love them, they all fall for that". The crazy part is as men we all gave girls false hope just cause we wanted some ass. To know what love really is , is simple . To actually practice it is very difficult. Adam and Eve love . The greatest love story ever told . Because of this story i know what true love is . They always talk about eve eating the fruit but why do you think Adam ate it? The real reason is he knew eve ate the fruit and because eating the fruit she will die , but his love for her was sooo strong he would rather eat it and die with her then to live eternity without her. That's deep love real love , love that puts someone else before your own feelings and happiness. Fake love is all about self enlightenment and assurance real love is selfless and understanding. Always try to differentiate

the two cause that's where your happiness
lies

VINDICTIVE

....

In all walks of life, you will find that one person, or perhaps a few that hold vindictive personality disorders. It's really not hard to avoid, heck I'm no expert psychologists and have not been trained to see signs in people before it's too late .

If you are anything like me, you always want to see the best in people. You understand that no person is perfect, and that they often are dealing with their own demons that come out in force when they feel that they don't have 100 percent control over a situation.

A vindictive person has misguided pain. They feel frustrated, helpless, hurt or ignored and are unable to change their circumstances without ensuring that they affect others in the meantime.

They don't have the necessary strength inside to find better ways to handle their feelings. I

Instead, they lash out and convert pain into anger and seek revenge by taking that pain out on others.

Most commonly, they want to bring others down with them. They feel by using the power of manipulation, they are able to not have to experience the misery by themselves - they can in fact bring others in. I've seen men hold grudges over high school sweethearts someone stole from them or even small hood beef that's gotten a couple people merked

A person that's bitter builds grudges, stores pain points against themselves and others to justify their feelings. It's always someone else's fault and you will never find them in a situation where they will apologize. They don't realize that they cannot harm others without harming themselves, and not only come unstuck in their personal lives but also in their careers.

If something doesn't go their way, they attempt to intimidate you or manipulate you. They will throw out lines to try and scare you, and if they are in.

Once you become a target, a vindictive person will try and destroy you. They need to prove you are the ultimate loser by destroying you. Unfortunately in this day and age, there is the internet - a perfect forum for people with vindictive personality disorders to play out their anger or pain, and try and cause reputational damage among other types of damage.
You ever see a guy post a girl nudes on Facebook or girl screenshot a message of someone and put them on blast for millions of people to see? That's the things now that a vindictively person would do. Where I'm from Philly , almost every girl is vindictive, they save text threads. Just so one day they can screenshot or send it to someone, i don't blame them but we live in a world where revenge means more then walking away.

What we haven't realize do the is that "anger, revenge, and harassment comes from a place of weakness" and eventually they will burn those around them, and ultimately themselves.

The best ways to manage a vindictive person is:
- Don't buy into their gossip or attempts to turn you against another person
- Encourage positivity and proactive approaches to life
- Disengage with vindictive and negative people - they will only destroy your mojo as well as the person that is their target
- See the signs as early as possible, and realize that there is no place in your life for people like this

LETTER TO MY YOUNGER SELF

***

25 YEAR OLD LEONARD MEETS 35 YEAR OLD LEONARD

What's up Nostra? Congratulations on lj being born , no matter how much you think you can be doing better, you're doing a damn good job. This is you by the way writing this letter, well I'm sending it to my younger self The more we're exposed to in this world, the more we realize how little we know or understand. That said, please take what's useful from this advice and leave behind what is not. You will create your own journey which makes you unique.

I am not writing you in the hopes of swaying your decision. Altering the past can have grave consequences on the future. Perhaps the 35 year old self you come to be doesn't exist today if you choose otherwise. That is a risk that I am not willing to take

I can tell you one thing you're going to change lives .

you won't listen to the advice below. That's cause we already think we have life planned out but I'm going to give you some key bulletin points

- You're going to experience some amazing things. Humble yourself or the universe will do it for you.
- The world is much bigger than us and it doesn't revolve around us. The people we respect the most, including our mentors, are the humblest people we'll ever meet one will be extremely arrogant but hey... you'll humble yourself just to not be like him

- Continue to love the same way , your relationship with your kids mother may or may not work but don't never let anything stop you for caring for an individual.

- Your career is going to take off, but please, please don't get caught up. Make family a Priority you'll have other kids .Show up for family. It matters.

God is the best! , well you already know that , but fostering an early relationship with him can make our life way easier than it is now . Your sister is still crazy and your parents will be the two you learn to respect the most . Spend more time with them and peguiteau! .

Don't want to tell you too much but keep Doing your thang! We will meet again in another ten years take care

REJECTION

....

You can't control the way that somebody loves you. You also cant control when someone doesn't want a relationship and you do, it can be hard to detach from that person. But if this is the situation you are finding yourself in right now, you need to leave them so that you can pursue the relationship you desire. You owe yourself that. you're not going to be able to change what you want to suit them. Disregarding how you feel is only making you have resentment in the end

Frustration and disappointment was something i went through when i realized that I was not going to get what I wanted. Feelings of rejection or disbelief might be heightened when it seems like the both of you would be compatible in every way except . But the truth of the matter is that if someone doesn't want a relationship, then the two of you aren't compatible.

Don't let the concept of time dictate how meaningful your relationship was to you. Some people date for years without ever arriving at a level of true intimacy; sometimes, the most divine intimacy is experienced between two people who never dated at all. feelings of hurt and frustration are totally valid, shorty ain't want me and i was questioning my swag .. but then i recognized the fact that my crush never set out to do wrong to me made me really come to the conclusion she really wasn't on that time with me . We chilled spent hours and kissed But i wasn't worthy of a title and nobody owes me a relationship. In causing my heartbreak, she was teaching me a valuable lesson of rejection and i closed my heart. We all know that finding your soulmate is like finding a needle in a haystack these days

PLANTING SEEDS IN A CHILD

....

My heart is and mind is just blown for the
loss of parenting skills in this generation of
young people who have become parents.
They have not learned God's Word, so

they do not understand His directives in
the "How To" of the seeds they plant as
they mold their children.

I believe that much of the child's molding
will take place during the first five years of
his life. Therefore, it is imperative to plant
the seeds in this precious young child that
will produce the greatest harvest.

I often see young children who "talk back"
to their parents with no understanding of
the disrespect they are doing : they have
not been taught the meaning of respect. At
these times, it is very evident to me that
the parents have not been consistent in
their "seed planting." Allowing children to
be wild and free is a great disservice to
them. Requiring respect provides
wonderful security for them to trust and
rest in their parent's decisions as they grow
older. This will also have a great impact on
those to whom they will go with their
fears, problems, and concerns later in life,

as well as, whether or not they will have respect for the laws where ever they go.

Many times, Parents say "pick our battles." With your kids Perhaps, for some this works, though I do not feel that it holds true. Growing up Haitian , my mom would whoop my ass just looking at her the wrong way or talking back . Even though me and my siblings got discipline we knew who held authority and the best interest for us , and that was our parents . The relationship was healthy and it was also well needed .If the relationship between the parent and child is healthy and positive, as it should be, then there will be mutual respect with fewer battles and respect for those in authority. I am not implying that by raising your child in this manner, there will be no trials, only that it will be a more joyful and problem thinking in their journey.

Growing up my parents never smoked, did drugs or never put me around where negative things were the norm. When i was in my teens my friends smoked weed but i never did because it never interested me , nice cars fast money or any thing gloried negativity didn't appeal to me and still till this day I'm a boring chilled guy, thanks for the seeds my parents planted in me . When lj was born (my first son) i said to myself "He must have a great deal of his parents' attention and time", so that bonding, which brings forth security and trust, is established. The most important principle in this process is consistency. My "yes" must mean "yes," and "no" mean "no"! Otherwise, the son can easily become a manipulator. I gave my three boys the same consistency and I'm not saying their going to be saints or goody two shoes but what i instilled in them will forever show no matter what good or bad they do

KEEPING IT A BEAN

....

Do you keep it real with yourself? You probably are having a hard time answering this question because you know you are not or aren't sure what being honest with yourself really means.

The truth is human beings are hard-wired to create the perfect impression of themselves even when things aren't right. I don't know why but, maybe it's due to over-confidence, under-confidence, self-deception, or prototype effects. But lying to yourself makes things worse and this affects your long term positivism. It's crazy that most of us don't abide by this principle and we often find ourselves struggling with pessimism, negative mind-set, lack of ambition, feeling submerged in a life of negativity and much more. Being honest with yourself is key to living your life to the full. Not only does it have positive impact on yourself but also to people around you. Being honest allows you to have a positive mindset even when life throws lemons at you, and instead of "running to the hills," you gather up courage and face the problem by making "lemonade."

Honesty also helps you detect self-deception that we use smokescreen. Many people abide by the "Fake it till you make it" ruler . They will be in a relationship that has been dead for years, will take flowers to a colleague in hospital yet they despise him/her, will sing praises to their annoying boss, or will get married just because society says so even when they don't want to. All these situations are fake and will have negative effects. You will despise your spouse, hate being married, dislike your colleague or boss, hate your job and most critical you will be destroying your soul.

By your own soul, learn to live and if men thwart you take no heed. If men hate you have no care. Sing your song, dream your dream, hope your hope and pray your prayer.

Being like that is hard. You constantly need to evaluate your situations, accept reality and always work hard to remain true to yourself. At times you will have to make hard and life-changing decisions such as filing for divorce so as to get back your life and self confidence, letting go of a promising career that was draining you physically or emotionally, or even cutting links with your friends who may be derailing you. The only way to speak the truth is to speak lovingly. You can always handle the negativity in a positive manner without hurting others or secluding oneself. After all, positivism is infectious and will spread to those around . Maya Angelou when she said "A bird doesn't sing because it has an answer, it sings because it has a song."

Being honest with yourself isn't easy and doesn't take place overnight. It requires lots of dedication, willpower, sacrifice and patience. However, its benefits both short-term and long-term will outweigh the struggles and sacrifices. Not only will you enjoy longer term peace of mind and greater positivity but by being honest you also change the world around you. "A pessimist sees the difficulty in every opportunity; an optimist sees the opportunity in every difficulty." – Winston Churchill

SUICIDE

It's often difficult to imagine what led your homie , family member, or celebrity to commit suicide. There may be no warning signs, and you may wonder what clues you might have missed. Often, many factors combine to lead to a decision to commit suicide. It is often an act made during a storm of strong emotions and life stresses rather than after careful consideration.

While there are many factors which can influence a person's decision to commit suicide, the most common one is that the person has depression . A person is feeling great emotional pain but isn't able to see any way to relieve that pain other than ending her own life.

I felt hopeless before. I had aspirations and goals in life that didn't go my way and i didn't know how to handle it. Weather, it's individually successful goals , relationships or just losses of people around me made me feel empty and i wasn't worth life.

When a person feels that he or she has lost all hope and they don't feel able to change that, it can overshadow all of the good things in her life, making suicide seem like a viable option. While it might seem obvious to an outside observer that things will get better, a person with depression may not be able to see this due to the pessimism and despair that go along with this illness.

They're are single moms , and fathers that go trough this spell too, and i want to tell you , your not alone . I too after being away from my children's mother that's my life was over, i was a loser and my kids and the world would be better without me, no matter what people say or how others tried to cheer your existence. I smiled in their face while i was hurting inside the "woman, the life , and the career i always wanted is gone.. why am i still here!

In all my despair. I always felt god was with me . Old scriptures would always play in my mind. Proverbs 22:6 (GNTA) Teach children how they should live, and they will remember it all their life.

My mother and father told me not to be a quitter and the most funny thing is , even in all my misery i was talking to god like he was my diary .

This much I can tell you – hard times are going to come your way. Grief, pain, anger, disappointment, hurt, tears – you'll face them all in this lifetime.

I wish I could promise you otherwise, but my life story bears the truth of what I've just said. You will face the death of people you love, you will find yourself lost in the abyss, you will be betrayed by those closest to you, and you will go through periods of devastating self-doubt but rest assure life does get better and there is a reason why you're here. Maybe it's for you to tell a story just like me !

To be continued……….

Made in the USA
Middletown, DE
11 April 2023

28544673R00047